For Your Garden

GARDEN GATES AND ARCHES

For Your Garden

GARDEN GATES AND ARCHES

TERI DUNN

FRIEDMAN/FAIRFAX

PUBLISHERS

DEDICATION

For MaryJane, who has created and continues to nurture a wonderful garden behind redwood gates; for Jay Smith—I hope you get to do *your* gates book!; for Bill and Laura Frase (Hon. Grandparents), who sent *The Secret Garden*; and for Shawn, Wes, and Tristan, with all my love.

ACKNOWLEDGMENTS

Special thanks to Lola Stanton! And thanks, as always, to Susan Lauzau.

A FRIEDMAN/FAIRFAX BOOK

©2000 by Michael Friedman Publishing Group, Inc.

Library of Congress Cataloging-in-Publication Data available upon request.

ISBN 1-56799-924-7

Editors: Susan Lauzau and Hallie Einhorn
Art Director: Jeff Batzli
Designer: Jennifer Markson
Photography Editor: Erin Feller
Production Managers: Ingrid McNamara/Leslie Wong

Color separations by Fine Arts Repro House Co., Ltd.
Printed in Hong Kong by Midas Printing, Ltd.

1 3 5 7 9 10 8 6 4 2

For bulk purchases and special sales, please contact:
Friedman/Fairfax Publishers
Attention: Sales Department
15 West 26th Street
New York, NY 10010
212/685-6610 FAX 212/685-1307

Visit our website:
www.metrobooks.com

Contents

INTRODUCTION

A gate is the threshold of a garden. It is a doorway to a sanctuary, a border between the world out there and the world in here, an invitation, a beginning to a story. If you are poised to install a garden gate, stop and ponder your choice with great care. The decision is an important one, as this feature will have a powerful effect on both the demeanor and practicality of your garden.

The right gate expresses a garden's character. This entrance should be in harmony with not only the fence it may be a part of, but also the plants beyond. An old-fashioned white picket gate promises an informal setting or a quaint cottage garden. A more contemporary design, perhaps fashioned from metal or sleek cedar, hints at exciting, nontraditional plants and ideas.

Naturally, a gate is meant to be functional. It should comfortably admit you and your guests, plus any gardening equipment you favor—from an ordinary wheelbarrow to a rototiller or riding mower. You might also want the gate (and an accompanying fence, arch, or arbor) to be a physical barrier against noise and intruders, animal as well as human. While see-through gates may seem inviting, they can also constitute a security risk that you may not be willing to take. In any event, it is generally best if your gate swings inward, keeping it in the domain of the garden and—most importantly—leading arrivals inside.

Your choices in the realm of gates are many. Instead of the traditional wooden or metal gate, you might consider an open entrance, which often takes the form of an archway. Such an entry deftly combines frankness with mystery. And the now-popular arbor and gate sets allow the entrance to become part of the garden itself.

The following pages not only present a vast range of gate options, varying in terms of style and material, but also show how these features can be seamlessly incorporated into different types of gardens. So go forth and choose well!

ABOVE: Red brick and clay dominate this courtyard, so the gardener wisely chose a dramatic contrast for the gate. The powder blue paint gives the eye a refreshing break from the reddish brown hues and prevents the area from seeming too oppressive. Left ajar, the little gate almost seems to spring open, graciously coaxing visitors to enter.

OPPOSITE: When the plant choices in a garden are not overly complicated, an intricate metal gate really lends a sense of style. Such a gate also works beautifully with gravel or flagstone-based courtyards, because the light hues of the stones throw the detailing into relief. The embellishment at the top of the gate is reminiscent of a peacock's feathers—a design that suggests the owners take great pride in their garden.

ABOVE: A garden with a casual, meandering layout is well served by an informal, trellislike gate. The gate's patterned design helps preserve the sense that a gardener's hand is at work here, while the rough, twiggy texture harmonizes with the plant life beyond. The natural-looking material echoes the slatted roof of the distant gazebo.

ABOVE: This archway of woven fibers introduces visitors to a temperate garden. Thanks to the material, the structure exudes a tropical air consistent with the plantings. Useful as well as atmospheric, the entry offers a patch of soothing shade and gracefully weathers outdoor conditions in the mild climate. Notice, too, how well the structure has been absorbed by its site; shrubs, vines, and palms have all been encouraged to embrace it from the sides.

RIGHT: Considerable effort went into constructing this arch, fashioned from pliant hazel stems in such a way as to give it a loose, carefree demeanor. Scarlet runner beans (*Phaseolus coccineus* 'Painted Lady') provide quick, easy coverage along the sides. Meanwhile, the upper portion of the bower is left bare to create a window to the treetops and sky. Owing to the fragility of the arch and the fact that the beans are perennial only in mild climates, this scheme is best emulated in areas with snowless winters.

ABOVE: When choosing a gate, it is often wise to consider what is inside and outside the garden. While this garden features a cultivated border of purple and yellow perennials, the area on the other side of the gate abounds with wildflowers. The white picket gate is a fitting choice, since it gives a similar impression of both order and informality. Moreover, the generous spaces between the slats allow visitors to enjoy the untamed beauty of the field from within the garden.

LEFT: Everything about this gate is alluring, from its open slat design, which filters sunlight and beckons visitors onward, to its crisp, bright whiteness, which glows against the dark hedge. Composed of two doors that are mirror images of each other, the gate echoes the striking symmetry of the plantings.

LEFT: When a garden seems more like an outdoor room, as is the case with this brick-lined courtyard, a gate that reminds one of the door to a home is a natural choice. This beauty features carved detailing that is a decorative equal to the formal purple blossoms of the potted agapanthus plant just inside.

ABOVE: Even in winter, the complete harmony of this landscape is apparent. From the picket fence and accompanying arch to the Adirondack chairs and the birdhouses of cabinlike design, the area has a rustic feeling. The arch not only marks the entrance, but also breaks up the repetition of the fence's lines.

ABOVE: Here is an outstanding example of an entryway carved out of a manicured hedge. As with any formal hedge, the gardener's clippers must be employed often during the growing season to maintain the outline and neatness of the design. But the extra effort is well worth it, as there is nothing quite like being ushered through such a majestic living portal. Tall, potted white tulips stand at attention on either side of the path to form an elegant receiving line.

OPPOSITE: Matching textures define this setting. The brick arch and brick path below it provide a common backdrop for a cheery array of flowers. This design scheme is especially useful for those who favor a wide variety of flowers in the garden yet feel that a unifying factor is desirable.

ABOVE: A strikingly modern gate made of metal panels greets visitors at a Swiss garden. The whimsically placed windows, which provide eye-catching views of hearty geraniums, banish any sense of exclusion and promise that the landscape within will be sunny and lively.

ABOVE: A metal gate can be every bit as charming as a wooden one. If it comes unpainted or looks too plain, spend a few hours trimming it. Just be sure to use a high-quality, glossy, weather-resistant paint intended for metal surfaces so that it will retain its luster for at least a few seasons. This playful gate pays homage to its more common counterparts with a colorful array of finials.

Chapter One

WOODEN GATES

*T*he wooden gate is a garden icon—and with good reason. Many fences are made of wood, and it often makes sense to have the entryway composed of the same material as the rest of the structure. Wood also looks appropriate and natural; the wood that was once a tree is now a contributor to a planted landscape. And then there is the tactile element. Rough or smooth, painted or left bare, wood always feels solid, substantial, and durable. If you spring for expensive cedar, it even smells good.

Once you have decided on wood for your entrance, there are many options to consider, depending on your taste and budget. Redwood, cypress, and black locust are strong, decay-resistant woods, but they can be pricey and are not available everywhere. Pine and fir are softer, less expensive choices. Other possibilities include oak, Douglas fir, and hemlock. Visit a lumberyard to see what you like, even if you intend to install a manufactured gate.

Many woods weather over time, helping the gate, archway, or fence settle into the scene. The dove gray of aged cypress is especially handsome, imbuing the surroundings with a serene air. Of course, any wood's appearance can be enhanced, and its life extended, with wood preservatives, stain, or a coat of paint. One advantage to using paint is that this substance provides the opportunity to establish charming color vignettes with the flowering plants in the garden beyond. It also allows you to inject vital energy into an otherwise monotone setting. White is a classic choice that "goes with" everything, but what if you opted for periwinkle blue and grew a shell-pink rose next to the gate?

ABOVE: The sere, tan tones of an adobe wall and its attendant pottery are relieved by a vibrant shade of blue for the entrance. To keep the doors in harmony with the rustic surroundings, the gardener has allowed the paint to weather. Still, the hue retains its radiance and calls to mind the sea, hinting that a lush oasis lies beyond the threshold.

OPPOSITE: This casual picket fence–style gate presents something of a surprise, considering the formal company it keeps. Flanked by handsome clipped and trained greenery and approached by a classic flagstone path, the gate sports a coat of blue paint—another unorthodox touch for the setting. The design casts an air of intrigue, leading one to wonder if other tradition-breaking combinations await inside the garden.

ABOVE: An imaginative design can confer beauty and character on even the plainest wood. This gate's weatherbeaten, untreated timbers were the object of careful craftsmanship—note the smooth, symmetrical curves, the way the evenly set slats are neither too slight nor too thick, and the graceful effect of the neatly dovetailing lower boards.

OPPOSITE: Matching taller perennials, such as these phlox, echinops, and campanula, to gate height creates a powerful sense of accord. Wooden planking is a good choice because it does not clash with the flowers in terms of color or form—the unadorned, smooth surface looks great with everything.

ABOVE: A wooden gate—particularly a weathered one—is an ideal choice for an herb garden, as the aged appearance works well with plants that are rich in history and folklore. Here, the fossil designs foster the impression that both the gate and the freshly planted herb garden it protects have been around for eons.

OPPOSITE: If rustic appeal is what you desire, salvage sturdy old wood where you can and rig together the gate of your dreams. In this peaceful setting, the gate proves to be an agreeable companion for a wall of stacked stones bearing the same hues and unrefined demeanor as the wood. The enchanting cottage garden beyond is framed perfectly.

ABOVE: This gate acts as an effective link between the garden and the house, thanks to an invigorating coat of blue paint that matches the color of the window frames and mullions. The bold hue also provides welcome contrast to the pastel pink hollyhocks.

RIGHT: These big, blowsy rhododendrons would easily overwhelm the garden's entrance were it not for diligent pruning and a well-chosen gate. Despite the tightly packed blooms, the gate creates an airy feeling, thanks to its height, which is a good deal lower than the tall shrubs, and its generously spaced slats, which practically beg visitors to peek inside. With a sizable window of space between its base and the brick walkway, the gate appears to be floating magically.

ABOVE: Wider entries call for broader gates, and double gates prove to be an excellent solution. Dividing the entry space by using two doors helps retain a sense of intimacy. This handsome example includes heavy-duty posts, boards, and latch hardware, yet it never overwhelms, thanks to the double-door construction and see-through design.

ABOVE LEFT: Here, a double gate marks a vast entrance onto a sweeping lawn. The concave or "half-moon" top swings the focus toward the center where the gate opens and also cradles the view of the house beyond. In keeping with the rural setting, the lower portion of the gate resembles the styling found on many barn doors.

ABOVE RIGHT: When a garden brims with lavish greenery and carefully orchestrated perennial borders, an unpretentious wooden gate is ideal because it will quietly perform its service without competing with the surroundings. Here, such a gate is nestled beneath a bower of honeysuckle (*Lonicera*) and attended by rhododendrons. The overall scene makes you want to tiptoe in with a watering can or slip in early in the morning with a mug of hot tea.

ABOVE LEFT: An old stone wall with an archway requires a gate that not only fits the space but also varies the view. This wooden door fills the bill by supplying contrasting color and an open window to the landscape beyond.

ABOVE RIGHT: Here's a novel idea: the gate responds not so much to the plants as to the hardscape elements, from the café table and chairs to the rounded patio. Curves appear in the design of the gate, as well as in the individual split branches that make up the vertical slats. The feeling of being completely embraced by the garden is hard to resist.

OPPOSITE: Such cottage-garden favorites as wallflowers (*Cherianthus*) and forget-me-nots (*Myosotis*) billow around a slatted wooden gate. The gate's straight lines act as a strong foil for the flowing blooms, while the striking white color brightens up the commanding brick wall.

ABOVE: Many fences and walls in the American Southwest are constructed of thick, warm-colored adobe, made from indigenous clay. However, it is impractical to fashion gates from the same material. This gardener's solution is a wooden gate of deep, earthy brown that blends with the surrounding structure. By decorating all components—the wall, overhead arch, and door surfaces—with native images, the owner achieves an integrated whole.

ABOVE: This scene is a riot of textures and colors, with its brick pillars and pathway, the tan adobe wall, and the verdigris finish on the lantern-style lights, not to mention the exuberant growth of Shirley poppies (*Papaver rhoeas*). The worn wooden gate contributes to the excitement, presenting yet another surface and color to admire.

Chapter Two

METAL GATES

There's just something so romantic, so classic, about a garden gate that is fashioned from metal. Whether of wrought iron, steel poles or panels, copper tubing, or a combination of these, a metal gate can be quite ornate and formal in creative hands. It also has the potential to project a modest and inviting appearance.

You can purchase a metal gate from a gardening catalog, garden-themed shop, or even some hardware stores. But if the gate does not need to be in mint condition, a salvaged one can be an exciting alternative. If you're lucky, you'll find a charming old one tucked away in some rural antique shop or at an estate sale. With a little cleaning and fixing, and perhaps some new latching or hanging hardware, a rescued gate can become a garden treasure.

Metal gates also boast the advantage of longevity—no rotting, no breaking down, no leaning. Looking like they have been solidly in place for ages, they endure the years stoically while the garden matures around them. Eventually, they may show some slight wear and tear, if only in a few dents or spots of rust—testimony to seasons of exposure and years of people and equipment passing through their portals. A coating of oil, oil-based or enamel paint, or a steel powder or galvanized finish will help sustain the surface.

ABOVE: Although a wide and substantial gate has the potential to be ungainly, this one bears a lacy design that gives it a delicate quality. The fanciful curlicues hide little of the garden, which tempts wanderers with its verdant scenery and flourishing blooms.

OPPOSITE: A gate of black forged-iron bars is an inspired choice for a garden whose most salient resident is a flowering cherry, because the trunk and branches of this type of tree are especially dark in color. Both the tree and gate gain a sculptural quality from their juxtaposition. Stone pots of produce perched atop the brick pillars hint at the delicious fruits of the garden.

ABOVE LEFT: Thanks to the mature trees and draping, flower-laden stems of the climbing rose, this garden appears to be well established. Yet the undisciplined growth of the gray-leaved lamb's ears (*Stachys*) and rosy-flowered valerian (*Centranthus ruber*) suggests that the gardener is not overly fussy or meticulous. The metal gate reinforces this relaxed sense of refinement with its clean lines.

ABOVE RIGHT: Formal settings call for formal gates. No wooden gate could ever provide the elegance that this metal entrance confers upon the sculpted elements within, from the regal stone pedestal to the highly refined, clipped boxwood and yew hedges in the distance. The darkness of the metal modestly keeps the focus on the garden itself, allowing the gate to retreat into the shadows.

OPPOSITE: Again, formal, dense hedges find a perfect mate in a dignified metal gate. This one sports an ebullient scroll design that displays a bit of whimsy, yet remains in keeping with the garden's stately character.

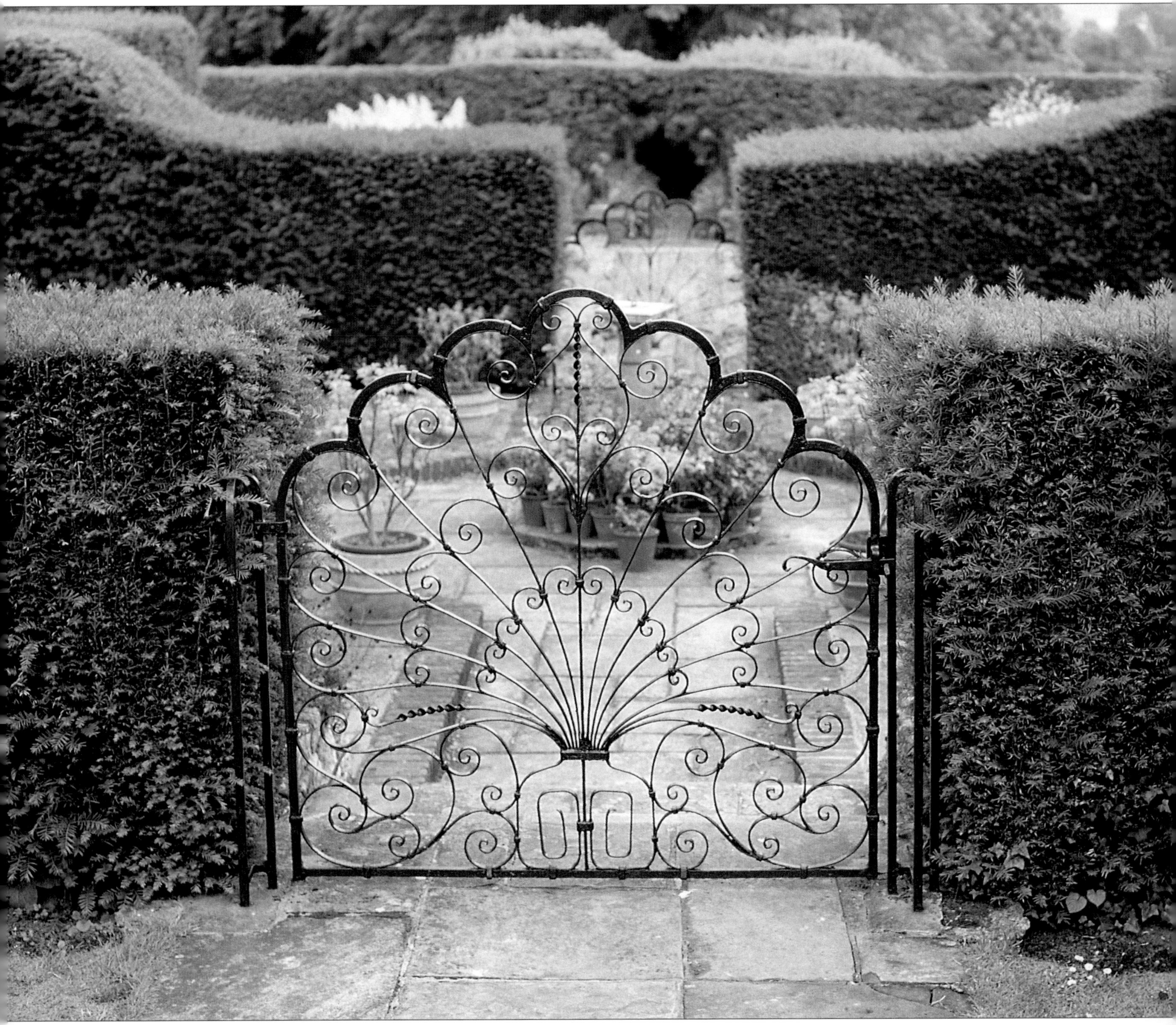

ABOVE: This classic, straightforward metal gate is actually no more than an extension of the fence. This type of setup works particularly well in a garden that is small or hemmed in by adjacent gardens. The fluid, no-nonsense design results in less distraction, thereby preventing the scene from seeming too busy.

OPPOSITE: Courtyards are well served by metal gates—the garden is still enclosed, but any feeling of confinement or claustrophobia is diminished. This gate bears a combination of curves and lines that creates the same airy impression as the transom above the front door. With its plain, solid posts and unpretentious design, the gate reflects the tone of the Japanese-style urban courtyard.

LEFT: A metal gate is a wonderful partner for a brick wall. Here, such a gate allows visitors to see in, as well as out, providing respite from the bricks' imposing nature. Upbeat alstroemerias in the foreground gain warmth from the coloring of the brick backdrop, even as they spring outward to meet those who enter.

OPPOSITE: A busy cottage garden, overflowing with roses and trellised sweet peas, is flattered by a dainty metal gate. While the gate's central pattern shares the lighthearted feeling of the garden's design, the frame consists of bold geometric shapes that imply the gate means business. The structure's airy styling helps open up the snug space, and its curving lines echo the delicate arms of the rose-colored bench.

LEFT: There is nothing terribly ornate or overbearing about this gate—nor is the design bluntly floral. Yet the way in which the metal pieces rise from the base and swirl upward and outward mimics the growth of the shrubs and flowers. The heart shape at the center of the composition extends a warm welcome and suggests that the garden is cherished.

RIGHT: This spare yet attractive iron gate is similar to the climbing rose it supports in that it boasts inherently elegant lines adorned with flourishes of beauty. Note that the arch is actually part of the frame and always remains solidly in place, providing stability for the roses so that they are not disturbed when the gate is opened. A flower design at the top keeps this garden in bloom year-round.

ABOVE: When you are installing a wall or fence at the same time that you are choosing the gate, you have the perfect opportunity to make a perfect fit. This situation is particularly beneficial when you are dealing with a metal gate, which cannot be whittled an inch or two here and there! This iron gate, painted white to give it an uplifting look, comes with its own metal arch to hang and swing from—a nifty way to ease the tricky problem of attaching hinges to stone.

ABOVE: A handsome wrought-iron gate emerges next to a billowing perennial border, bringing order and an element of constancy to the garden. The green lawn glimpsed beyond provides natural windows of color between the gate's black lines. Boosted by a stone step, the gate is slightly elevated, lending the garden an air of importance.

OPPOSITE: If you are enchanted by this gate, consider seeking out an enterprising metalsmith to forge one for your garden. You could even provide the old tools, salvaged perhaps from the garage, a junkyard, or an antique barn; they certainly don't need to be in working condition and probably shouldn't be sharp, for safety's sake. In the end, you'll have quite a conversation piece.

RIGHT: If your garden is less than colorful or the bloom time is relatively brief, a festive gate can fill the void. This handcrafted gate of folk-art design provides a point of interest and constant color throughout the seasons. Naturally, botanical themes work particularly well in this type of situation.

ABOVE: Note how the unadorned architecture of this gate secures the doorway without stealing the show from the decorative wall accents and the antique urn overhead. Planted with greenery, the urn allows the garden to become part of the entrance.

OPPOSITE: Mediterranean gardens go hand in hand with iron gates, which admit plenty of warm sunshine and breezes. This gate has the added advantage of slender bars and finial-inspired tops that echo the fan-trained vines mounting the wall. Tiles crowning the arch enhance the Mediterranean look and lend an air of distinction.

Chapter Three

OPEN ENTRYWAYS

*I*f you have adventurous taste and security is not a factor, consider an unorthodox choice: the gateless entryway. This type of passage is often an archway of some kind, and with careful consideration of the materials, placement, and adjacent plantings, it can be quite extraordinary.

The trick is to get such an entryway into place as early as possible in your garden's development. That way the structure can easily be incorporated or enveloped by the surrounding plants, and a harmonious environment can be achieved. If this strategy is not possible, you can clear a broad area, longer and wider than the proposed entry, and landscape the site anew. The success of the scheme rests on how well you are able to integrate the entryway with the garden. As many people find out the hard way, wedging an archway or the like into the midst of existing plants is not a particularly easy task.

Some entryways are composed entirely of plants, such as massive, twining vines or sculpted hedges. Others are pure hardscape, fashioned from brick, stone, wood, or other non-living materials. But an entrance that mixes these concepts, such as a rose-draped wooden arbor, is perhaps the most desirable. The support defines the opening, while the plant announces that a garden lies ahead.

ABOVE: This Japanese-influenced garden is approached through a graceful, moonshaped entrance, which deftly frames the view and contributes to the overall theme of geometric shapes within the garden. The roundness of the entry has a nurturing effect, embracing those who pass through on their way to the peaceful setting beyond. Had an actual gate been installed in this opening, the flow would have been obstructed and the serenity lost.

OPPOSITE: As a stone path winds its way into the garden, a stone archway pitches in with a harmonizing note. To keep the massive entrance from seeming too imposing, the gardener has incorporated a delicate honeysuckle vine that provides a lighthearted touch of greenery and fragrance.

ABOVE LEFT: An intertwined grapevine and copper arch imbue this garden with a sultry feeling. The match remains beautiful throughout the seasons, as the leaves change from green to red to soft yellow against the metal's handsome finish. (Ultimately, copper left outdoors gains an appealing aquamarine patina, which alters the color combinations but is no less lovely.) A mural on the back wall tricks the eye into thinking that the cozy garden is much larger than it actually is.

ABOVE RIGHT: An archway of flowers is this gardener's idea of an inviting entrance. Since a climbing rose cannot be trained into this shape on its own, support is provided by stakes of willow, a strong but flexible wood. A rose with especially pliant canes is a wise choice for this type of setup. Here, repeat-blooming 'New Dawn' fills the bill.

OPPOSITE: The artistic hand of the gardener is evident here in every detail, from the dazzling path to the painted wooden beds to the daring color combinations in the flower borders. The entrance, too, transcends the ordinary with a copper arch whose bold stars suggest that there is something out of this world about the garden. Nestled in the midst of this celestial crown, the white petals of a popular clematis hybrid called 'Ernest Markham' provide heavenly accompaniment.

ABOVE: If the first tree a visitor will see is one that blazes with color each autumn, as does this sweet gum (*Liquidambar styraciflua* 'Worplesdon'), a brick entrance offers an ideal frame. With its warm red and rust tones, the archway sets the stage for the colorful show to come.

RIGHT: A pergola can achieve the magical effect of an outdoor "hallway." When the beams are cloaked in foliage and flowers, the resulting shade provides soothing respite from the hot sun. The extensive length of the entrance creates a feeling of suspense as to what the garden holds in store.

ABOVE: Young trees can be trained to form an archway. This technique, perfected in European gardens, is called "pleaching," from the French *plechier,* meaning "to braid." Linden (*Tilia*) trees are used here, but other options include beech (*Fagus*), hornbeam (*Carpinus*), and even apple (*Malus sylvestris*), all of which have sturdy, flexible branches.

ABOVE: This striking entrance gives one the sensation of peering through an oversize keyhole. The effect is tantalizing, offering a generous peek at the world beyond, while at the same time casting an air of intrigue.

ABOVE: Postcard pretty, this rustic vine-cloaked arch hails visitors at an ambitious British garden. An actual gate, even one with bars or slats to see through, would have interrupted the smooth flow from the front flower borders to the show within. No doubt the gardener must keep the foliage and flowers on the arch itself in control, so that the entrance remains accessible.

OPPOSITE: With its substantial depth and sheltering configuration, this dramatic stone structure is reminiscent of a foyer. Marking the transition into the garden's sitting area, the archway announces a shift in gears. The open design, as well as the trompe l'oeil vines climbing along the walls inside, ensures that the garden remains a strong presence at all times.

ABOVE: Filling the air with romance, a rose-laden arbor is difficult to resist. The profuse blooms and dense foliage showering this one suggest that the garden has been thriving for many years. However, this bewitching effect can be achieved in a mere season or two by planting a pair of husky roses and pampering them with water, fertilizer, and if necessary, sprays.

OPPOSITE: This dramatic arbor boasts a series of arches, large and small—a design that keeps the eye engaged. The encircling pink roses exude a celebratory tone, as though there were a lively garden party or wedding on the other side.

Chapter Four

ARBOR AND GATE SETS

There is a growing trend these days toward buying and installing a gate that comes with a coordinating, overarching arbor. You can find these sets in a number of garden-supply catalogs and even at local nurseries that have sections devoted to garden decor. Generally, the structure comes unassembled, as a kit, complete with all the necessary hardware and detailed instructions. (Of course, if you don't feel up to the job, you can always get help from someone who is handy with construction projects.)

The advantages of these sets are many. Since the individual components are designed to go together, there's no awkward fussing and fitting—everything should snap neatly and sturdily into place. From an aesthetic point of view, they already work well together in terms of style, color, and proportion—with no effort on your part. And, last but not least, it is highly satisfying to erect a complete and beautiful garden entrance quickly.

But you don't have to go this route. You can make your own gate and arbor, or arch, set from plans you devise yourself or ones you find in a garden construction handbook (with modifications that suit your taste and your garden). Or you may be fortunate enough to find yourself with a garden that already has a gate or an arch, but not both, and decide to go ahead and put its mate into place.

One final note: a gate and an arbor or arch can be coordinated without bearing the exact same characteristics. A white wooden gate doesn't have to pair up with a white wooden arch, nor does a cast-iron gate require an arbor of the same material. After all, these structures are not operating in a vacuum. There is an entire garden to consider: plants already in place and those you intend to grow, pathways, and other hardscape elements. Peruse the examples in this chapter, take your cues from your garden, and install whatever seems right to you.

OPPOSITE: Echoing the home's framed doorway is this framed "outside doorway." Notice how the gate and arch combination permits the white climbing rose and other adjacent plants to grow freely without danger of their blocking the view. In a similar fashion, the entrance to the house plays host to casually draped pink blooms, while at the same time keeping the passageway easily accessible.

ABOVE: Here is a classic white wooden set, which you can buy as a kit and put together yourself. The color and style recall simpler times, when life was less hectic and time moved at a more relaxed pace. The setup, along with the calming view of the sea, sends the message that all worries and pressures must be checked at the door.

ABOVE: Since the tidy boxwood topiaries are meant to dominate this garden, the end of the allée is marked by a modest iron gate. But lest this feature be overlooked, a rose-covered archway has been added above it. The arch mimics the shape of the bushes and brings the entrance into scale with the garden.

OPPOSITE: This highly picturesque entrance is filled with wonderful touches. The concave gate meets with the overhead arch to form a vast, circular window into the garden. Emerald green accents artfully connect the man-made structure to the natural environment, while iron hardware adds a traditional flair.

ABOVE: This informal gate is made all the more friendly by the gingerbread-like design of the arch. The scalloped edges exude a fluid quality, creating the impression that they just might flutter gently in the breeze along with the leaves. The total picture makes you feel like bounding through the entrance to discover what treasures await in the garden.

LEFT: This entryway is a symphony of forms. Pointy, clipped evergreens echo the sharp finials on the fence, while an arch soars above them all in splendor. The ogee arch, topped by an abstract depiction of a tree, lends an exotic touch to the prim surroundings.

LEFT: While this hedge archway does not actually surmount the gate, it does deftly frame it. The setup elongates the garden's entrance, which is filled with a series of gradually descending steps. When designing the space, the gardener recognized the wisdom in simplicity and opted for a restrained, low wooden gate with slats to admit sunlight.

OPPOSITE: There was no better choice for this setting than a wooden gate, which maintains the natural look of the arching trees. The leafy tunnel (made of flexible hazel trees) selflessly extends shelter to those who pass through, causing guests to feel nurtured as they make their way to the garden. Note that the gate is not made of the same wood as the trees, but it works well because the thickness of its slats and supports is proportionate to the slender trunks.

ABOVE: In this enchanting design by landscaper Mirabel Osler, the arch and open gate provide a tantalizing glimpse into a sunny, flower-strewn setting. Even when the gate is closed, the alluring scene remains highly visible, thanks to the open crisscross pattern. The darkness of the wood makes the colors within the garden seem even more vibrant.

OPPOSITE: A birdbath and numerous low-growing plants are in good company with a low gate. The oft-used Z-construction is jazzed up by the inclusion of arching metal loops, which echo the shape of the clematis-filled arbor overhead.

ABOVE: A conventional Z-design wooden gate has met its match with a spare, geometric arch. Triangular in shape, the top of this arch is similar to the pediment of an interior doorway. The overall effect is decidedly "Western ranch," emphasized further by the addition of a period lantern.

ABOVE: The delicacy of this metal arch and gate set counterbalances the heaviness of the stone wall and the garden's dense box hedges. A climbing rose acts like a fine seasoning, preventing the entrance from seeming too bland by injecting a little zest. The overall effect is one of understated elegance, which ties in well with the formal setting.

RIGHT: Thick, lavish grapevines swoon over a bolstering wooden arch. The free-form design of the gate, composed of swirling branches, creates the illusion that this is not a gate at all, but rather a natural barrier of tangled growth.

PHOTOGRAPHY CREDITS

A-Z Botanical Collection Ltd.:
pp. 33, 43

©**R. Todd Davis:** p. 58

The Garden Picture Library: pp. 2,
6, 7, 11, 15, 16, 17, 18, 20, 21, 22,
23, 27 right, 28 left, 28 right, 29, 34
left, 35, 36, 38, 39, 42, 45, 46, 47,
48, 50 left, 52, 57, 59, 65, 66, 68, 70

©**John Glover:** pp. 9, 10–11, 14, 49,
52–53, 67

Houses and Interiors: pp. 8 right,
40, 41, 55, 56

©**Dency Kane:** pp. 69 right, 70–71

©**Marianne Majerus:** pp. 24, 34
right, 44, 50 right, 60, 62, 64–65,
69 left

©**Allan Mandell:** p. 62

©**Charles Mann:** pp. 8 left, 12, 19,
30, 31

©**Clive Nichols:** pp. 26, 27 left, 32,
37, 51, 54

©**Nance Trueworthy:** pp. 13,
24–25, 61